Going Head to Head

— Also by Wade Stevenson —

Ice Cream Parlors in Asia (as Steven Wade)

Beds

The Little Book of He and She

One Time in Paris (a memoir of the 1960s)

A Testament to Love & Other Losses

The Electric Affinities

The Color Symphonies

Flutes and Tomatoes (a memoir with poems)

Dear You (a memoir with poems)

Moon Talk

The Absence of The Loved

Songs of the Sun Amor

Going Head to Head

Wade Stevenson

BLAZEVOX[BOOKS]
Buffalo, New York

GOING HEAD TO HEAD
by Wade Stevenson

Published by BlazeVOX [books]

Printed in the United States of America

Interior design and typesetting by Geoffrey Gatza
Cover photo: The Seated Scribe, Ancient Egyptian art; c. 2450–2620 BCE. Louvre Museum. Paris.

First Edition
ISBN: 978-1-60964-354-6
Library of Congress Control Number: 2019952146

BlazeVOX [books]
131 Euclid Ave
Kenmore, NY 14217
Editor@blazevox.org

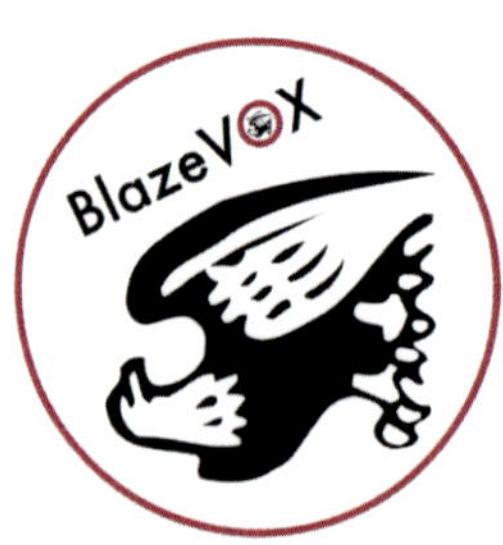

publisher of weird little books

BlazeVOX [books]

blazevox.org

21 20 19 18 17 16 15 14 13 12 01 02 03 04 05 06 07 08 09 10

To Lori and Annawade, from head to heart

To Gary —

With Best Wishes —

[illegible]

Table of Contents

Going Head to Head

The signification of the head is from the interior. That this is signified by the head is because the head is above the body, and as just said, by higher things are signified interior things. And besides, the interior things of man are in his head, for in the head are the beginnings of the senses and of language, and the beginnings are the utmost things, because from them the rest is derived.

—E. Swedenborg (1688-1772)

When I see a head from a great distance, it ceases to be a sphere and becomes an extreme confusion falling down into the abyss.

—Alberto Giacometti

First, how the head was formed, how it emerged,
Becoming conscious of itself, how it burst
Out of darkness into life until it streamed
With dark light. Because the head creates
A gap, it splits
Us into one world of memory patterns
Another of sensual amorous feelings
Thus we are balanced in our brain,
Torn between the inner and the outer,
Volleyed between the darkness and the light!
Through the head we encounter life,
Through the eyes awareness blossoms,
Lips give birth to the world of words
Until by the body we meet our loss.
Soon the irreplaceable head replaced
The hand, and soon the machine
Took over from the human. Then
The terrible deformations began,
The old mindful self lost in obscurity,
The head almost conquered by the dark of AI

Still, somehow it clung to a radiance
An effulgence, half-effaced, a whisper
Of tragic brilliance. Phantom lips. Eyes
Grown cold, gaping, the whole body shaking
Because it had forgotten how to touch the earth.

Little by little the contradictions appeared
The waves grew, the sea raged
As the icebergs melted. Lacerations bit
Into the cheeks. The darkness cracked, ridges
Cleft the chin. At night the mind dreamt
Only of animals. And things changed.
Man changed. Woman changed. And the head
Knew everything would change, knew the body
Would be altered by the restless
Turning over and constant loss of the land.
Sooner or later there would be a return
But for now the head bobbed on a stick, wavered,
The eyes flashed, sparkled, grew dim
Opioids tore the mind apart, it dangled
Like a kite plucked by the wind! And this was nothing new,
Think of all the suffering the years have been through —
The ears still echo with the soundless laments

You spent so much time looking for a rhyme
But one day God came and said, ‘It’s time!”
Then the darkness rushed down. In the plains
The animals had been stabbed.
SpaceX rockets landed on Mars and the moon.
No chance for love or simple understanding,
The eyes glazed like dead fishes, lips sealed
On a secret doom, while the nostrils
Sought to interact with far-flung scents of the past

Could the world be saved
By the fragrance of a biscuit dipped in tea?
Nothing was sure. No sooner was a certainty
Raised in place than it began to crumble.
Impossible to say the thing in itself,
To say flower, grass, tree
To strip the masks, to embrace
The pure nudity of a face, to say how or why
The brain reacts or is it the heart
That knows and glows, flares and goes
Riprap and mmm-ahhh!, the firefly blood
Pulsing while all the bare body does is bawl
And go pipi and sometimes fuck
While the mind, off leash, hunts private foxes

Close your eyes
You are now in the house of your memories
Enjoy the stay

It is morning
Waves of light wash over
The barnacled rocks
Of what you've left behind
You're even more alone
Because you've promised yourself
You won't look at a newspaper
Or open your cell phone
For at least a week

Of course your lips want to speak
It's normal for thoughts in your mind
Like clouds always to move
But relax, sit, back, accept the fact
Of the emptiness of every real thing
If you can hear just one bird singing
It's the same as many birds singing
If you can love one woman profoundly
It's the same as loving all women profoundly

Look how the sea beyond you shimmers
Your ears have so many green whispers
Your eyes are millionaires
So hold your monumental head high
Life has just begun, there is still hope
And death is just another part of time

Suck the juice of an orange
Inhale the light within
Crack an egg, split the seed
The future deeds you will sow
Are already stored in the head
Thoughts whirl as they slowly spin down
The drain of your brain
All the lost loves, the tossed aside regrets
Collect beneath the surface
Grow numb with the pain
Amazing then how out of the pan-
Gender glazed vessel of the body
There finally appeared
The flower of a face
Remembrance of a joy,
Moving flash of light
In a single watchful eye

There's actually no need to die
The mind is always birthing fantasies
It's called "staying alive"

My head is hurting now
I'll wait a little bit until the pain goes –
The joy of my pain —
Perhaps it never will
Even when deep in doubt
Your face comes to cover mine
You always hold my head in your hands

What I want is for my mind to be a mirror
So clear
That when I look into it
There's no reflection of myself

What is this thing called mind?
Why am I stuck in it
As in a circular room
No doors, no windows, no escape
I move around it
Always trying to find
The point from which it all began
And never able to

Whether on foot, on a bicycle,
Or even an imaginary plane
I just keep circling in circles
Until I am totally encircled, circled out
I've lost my identity, I'm a no-man,
A nomad in my own space,
Restlessly seeking a way out
Of the many-mirrored maze of mind

It's going to happen
It may never happen
What the hell do I care?

Let me blast open this boom box
Through which messages have been transmitted
Like echoes through all the caves and cliffs of time

How is it that the gonzo gears
Grinding inside the bones of the head
Can upshift the body's unthinking machine
Into the madness of a mindless moment?

From mind to body, from body to mind
Take your pick, who's on first?

Sometimes the body declines to function
The live wire head decides to play dead
Because what's the use of a used life,
Of a spent love cooked over twice?
Everything you once loved you must now refuse
To seek out even one phantom flower
From that past would be cruel memory abuse
Think of all that's been written over time
In the mythic mind's book of remembrances
The scars and wounds of what was loved in the flesh
Survive tattooed on the skin of the brain

To sing the glory of the eyes worn wafer-thin
Both the visions of the Damned and of the Holy one
Caught in the rushing tidewaters
Like a hurricane lamp, the consciousness of one Son
Burns in the hurricane night
There's only one person who can save you —
There's only one you —
How amazing to find yourself stranded on the shore,
Washed up but alive!

In the depthless depths a glimmer survives
The seashell ears echo every murmur of thirsting lips

The love we built will never collapse —
I swear, my darling lighthouse!

I may be splintered but I'm solid
I'm splendid even if I'm sad
I'm superb and oh so bad
And I love you even though what I once loved in you
Died a long time ago

Let me find a blanket to cover myself
I'm tired of sleeping outside
When the ancient ache ignites
I'm left to wonder what treasure
Might be buried in the mind womb that is mine

Your brilliant dark pupils stare fixedly ahead
Your cheeks pale and cool as polar ice

The keys to the self locked in the gold of time
As the body twists, I squirm and scream
How to find an escape route from the terrible dream?
Eject from the rut of the patterned routine?

What to do with myself? What to do with my head?

It will happen like this:

When the body, suddenly gutted with joy, says “too much”

The burned out brain bombed with bliss

Volcanic tremors jolting the spine

The earth slipping under your feet

And you’re suddenly conscious

Of the vaster multiplicities of things

In the garden of the mental emperor

The fatal nightingales continue to sing

Take the first moment of anything

Life beginning from scratch

A tabula rasa in your head

Except for death, what else do you desire?

From the moment of birth the hairless head

Seeks its own oblivion

Let me shut my eyes

Let the longed for darkness come

A terrorist knife can only do the killing

But even a detached head can still do the talking

In the garden of the mental emperor

The birds of non-being chirp

It's time, it's time

The executioner asked, "What's inside of an egg?"

The secret yoke and its protective albumen

"And how about your head?"

Twenty bones and thirty-two white teeth

Nerves, veins, arteries, ligaments

Hair, eyes, nose, lips that can speak

A terrorist knife can only do the killing

But even a severed head can still do the talking

Tell me, what can you do with a head?

You can attach it to a body, hunt dreams in bed

You can hold it in your hands like a trophy

You can contemplate the startled eyes

In fear and awe

If you love it you can caress the fine cheek bones

Dark shadows crease the anguished face

The nose stands out, white schism

What you can do with those eyes

Depends on the intensity of love that you feel

The higher the love, the deeper you touch the mind
Immersing yourself in the reality of a silence
That pre-exists thought or language

One day the sealed lips will open
The voice of the poet
Will make itself heard again in the land

Hold your breath, listen carefully
The stone statue of the Buddha head
Will tell you all you need to know about this unquiet world

The eyes are always looking ahead
Twin searchlights probing darkness
Seen from that perspective
The back of the head is basically dead

In the great silence of the planetarium
In that space between two ears
Neural stars move reflecting millions of years

The nose knife cuts the blunt air
Cleaving a space for all the unremembered
Fragrances, scents of the past, to live —
The very thought of you makes the head rich

What emerges from the intimate niches
Of a frozen mind, scintillating in a new day light?

Bringing a jolt to the electric heart
Silent lips open, yearn to speak
The tongue sticks out, joining the conflagration
With a well-earned grimace

If a love like this goes on any longer
I feel my neck may well spiral out of control

Babe, your artic blue eyes are so cool
I want to look through the sockets into your soul

On the horizon the face of the beloved
Shines with a thousand transparencies

We both know what our future hides
Think of a world without shadows or light
When dawn comes and tints the sky
Let me fingertip your cheeks again
Because I want you to be sun-kissed
Your lily head blooming, lips inhabited
By redolent violet

In the sweet spring time of our love
We escaped the monastery of the body's rules
The nudity of those nights still ripens

I take a stutter step in time
I mop my brow, I map my fate
I'm always afraid of moving too late
I know we can't go back to the Cycladic days
When we lived in a dream house
Without doors or windows
And with just one touch, a simple caress
We could do without
Lips, eyes, or ears

To the near and distant disasters
We opposed a vision of love
No need to talk, we could let our minds go empty
Filled with a wonderful awareness

On our little island we stared at a bottomless future

From the ocean depths a prophetic voice arose
"Stop thinking," it said
"When you know that you are no longer thinking
Life will begin again."

In the same way that a lake on a summer day
Seems to be captured by its own reflective brilliance
So you and I, together and alone, stand, rubbed
Out into clarity, is it any wonder that
As we lovingly look at each other
Our heads start to shine, a silver sheen?
Our eyes the mirror of what we are and wish to be

Look at these lips — they have sacrificed
A promise of passion
For the exactitude of a facial geometry
My face is square
Because when I first came out
My father made and lost a dare

There's not much to me now
Amor has flown
I'm bare as bone
My face just needs a feather
Like death, to lift me up and make me free

Let the loud light be gone
Into the coolness of long ago loves

Life to the living can be such a waste
The purple of loss is an acquired taste

The air hangs stubborn and dry
Come, cut my mental opacity
Like bread and cheese
I want to run further than my chin
Until I become one and in!

Riddle me this, riddle me that
There's no easy way
To explain the whatness of it all

My dummkopf head, my poor blind eyes
Tomorrow perhaps I'll go for a walk
I'll be elegant, wear a Borsalino hat
To keep the soul of my head
From flying off into the imaginary spaces
Of which it dreams so often

There's no way out, there's no way in
When I was born I saw death
And that's how life begins

So, from a sweet slit, comes a fragile flare

That is briefly and blissfully lit
Before the darkness comes again
And the head yields to the tricks of time

Remember how lustily you lived, hooked
On chance, on unrememberable
One night stands, "no foul, no harm"
Your smiling skull reveals its charm

To capture the purity of a head
The liquid darkness of two staring eyes

Even the mere fact of a nose —
In every way an astonishment
Where are the scents of the last thousand years?
Who keeps the roses of the past?

The nose surely knows
The only fragrance that matters
Is petalled in the knowledge of nowness

So the time has come for my face and I

To come face to face one last time
The question is asked: dear head,
Master of body and spirit
Can you turn over a new leaf?
But so many leaves have fallen away
In so many long leavings
The few leaves left won't have long to stay

The shadow of the clouds hangs heavy over me
Timor mortis conturbat me
The shadow of the clouds hangs heavy over me
Timor mortis conturbat me

Watch: the evidence of happiness lies
In the startling chemistries of the cortex
In the metaphysical shop of the brain
In the voices that long to tell
What a deaf God doesn't want to hear

Overhead the planes continue to circle and bomb
In the village square decapitated heads fixed on spears

If you could open your lips
If you could emit one single cry

But your ears throb with the detonations
No room for love or any plucked emotion

Bodies go whoosh as the air is sucked out
Where is old man Moses who made his people free?

A starving dog lifts his leg and pisses
On the stump of a burned out tree

The shadow of the clouds hangs heavy over me

This head, my head, your head
Her head, his head, our head
No one's head, everyman's head
But look out ahead, on the wall
Glares a mounted devil head
Some catastrophe before the fall
You may seek to get ahead
You may long to give God head
To unite with the great Godhead
With your ears on backwards
Your mind running in reverse
How can you ever have heard?
With eyes wide shut

How can you pretend to have seen?

If you want to live well

Befriend the galaxies reflected

In the nerve cells of your mind

At a certain time you touched my eyelids

And I stopped seeing

There was no need to see

You feather fingered my lips

And I stopped speaking

There was no need to speak

You cupped your hand over my ears

I heard my own blood pounding

How was it you got inside my head?

You lived in dreams behind my eyes

You sealed my nose so I couldn't breathe

There was no need to breathe

I was already breathing in and out with you

These cheeks curved, pink, flat with innocence

Head of the child, the one born to be

From the sacred conjunction

Of the man/woman, these little lips

Have yet to learn how to cry
Much less to scream, between the astonishment
Of the moment, the expectation
Of the horrors to come, oh how slowly
Time turns and the necklace of necessity
Finally rings the neck
How to forget those aqua blue eyes
Alert as squirrels, the skin soft, vanilla-smooth
And what green images sing, dance
Play to the tune of a hole-less flute in the head
Warm, deep glimpses stored in brain synapses
Have yet to emerge, aroused by the love
Of a woman into a stark, bursting radiance
My poor baby's head, clear as a mirror
Simple, bedazzled in the dreams of childhood
Unaware the fix is in, the future booby-trapped

Roman coin of a face
With both sides half-effaced
A memory of the nose and the eyes
Ravaged by eagles

Ravines sleep in the cheeks

As, full speed ahead,
The nimbus head marches toward death
In the somber blaze of its gold

All that the eyes have seen
Now exist in a dim remembered dream
The ears shaped like spoons
Every form born forecasts its doom
But "I exist" the head screams
As it fights its way free of the womb
There will be time enough for all the moments
That come and go, for glitzy glamour
And early hints of the dying day's gloom

Faithless head, mindless mind, my old friend
Shrunk with emotions, hurt by hawks
I want to wrap you in a handkerchief
Bathe you in the gauze of my silence
Carry you away like a flashlight
In the calm darkness of my soul's rucksack

If I could only dwell in the depths
Of my head, safe, my body
Always within my reach

It's better than thinking I might be a cloud
Untethered, dissolving, floating away
It's better than knowing I must return to clay

One day when you're finally grown up
Your balloon head no longer swollen with hopes
Dancing on a string, cut off at the source
You'll go back to what you were
You will hide behind your nostrils, inhaling
The scents of a past that will be never be past

You'll go head to head with your head
Seeking a way forward from under the cheeks
To the height of the eyes and how they remember
All the quick convulsions of love that they've seen

Once Amor came in the evening
Gently washed your forehead like a sponge

You couldn't get away, one less hiding place!
No way to evade the gentlest caress
Once you thought you could live on the blink of your lids
Laugh with the secret of your whispered lips
Your face inhabited by the fullness of light
Your brain singing silently

To the beat of the heart

But now? Now? Now?
Tell me, what do you see and how?

I'm troubled by my face
I'm drunk behind my brow
Where do I go? What should I seek?

It's no fun to play hide and go seek with phantoms
If you hammer my shoulders they'll honk with hope
My eyes yearn for black granite and howl for peace
Closing them, I'll put my trust in everything I can't see
I'll follow the dark, twisting paths of the mind's inner "I"

If I could escape the burden of consciousness
The revolving repetitions would soon start
To unspool themselves
The mindless mind
Detached from the earth-bound body
Would float, empty, free
Thoughts rising like shotgun birds
Fluttering in space, flying so high!
From the dead a design would have risen

So that, looking up, I would vision
The black marker smile of a "head" balloon

If mind and body could go separate ways
If lust and love, once married, were to splurge
On unequal identities, then what?
Capped with ice, thin lips struggle
To formulate a meaning
While from far away I can't stop hearing
That ghost woman murmuring
"Don't talk. Don't talk."

Hello girl. Hello, my odalisk lover. I love it when you laugh
You don't go into a trance. Songs of innocence
Run like a virus in your blood. Your eyelids never flicker,
Your head fixed in a stream of perpetual brilliance
When your red lips smile, an ache somewhere
Forgets to accentuate. What thoughts hoover
Behind those mischievous curls that hover
As your head falls forward into reality
Or tilts backward into a somnolent vigilance
Every pixel of your adored face
Sustains itself, sprayed with an equal illumination,

A perfect balancing act!
You are gold, soft and sweet as the light itself
No stain or shadow in your mind
So you sleep, so sleepily you smile, your head
Nourished by the sunlight in the air, fine!

But does that suffice? Can human love
Be forgiven for being less than enough?
On a Nefertiti neck the head turns
The planet revolves, the primal anguish returns

I was fucked when I was born
Or perhaps I was born to fuck
What the fuck does it matter?
Was there real love in that seminal act?
I dangle on the light of my mind
Like a man flailing on a rope
I'm thinking: this isn't. It never should have been.
Yet there it is. It was me and I am

When bombs break over the countryside
Clouds scattered, skies blasted

What else to cling to but an immediate presence
The eyes seeking to cope
To adjust to the full scope
Of the narrowing, ever-widening moment
Caterpillar-like the head rises
From the shell-shocked shoulders
Cleaving to what it sees
Light spills, stunning the eyes
The coming darkness has swept
All hope off this face
Ears tottering on the edge of nothingness
When will the mooring ropes break
When will the head slip
Away into totally unknown seas?
Its nature being to reach beyond itself,
To bring together inner and outer
To live somewhere in the pulsing center
God is one, let one be god, and let that one be me

The head will never yield to death in life
Or life in death, even a diamond skull
Can have metaphysical dreams
The head will not walk alone in darkness
The heroic head has a thousand faces
Each visage illumined, ethereal beams

Full of streaks, dot, dashes
The plus and minuses of so many loves
That have appeared, disappeared, re-appeared
Ask the eyelids: they know how to blink or close
Ask the nose: it knows how to tell
The fakes from the real red rose

Autumn evening: faces float in mists
Shadows glide through trees
I can't see the sky, of which I dream
Nor the earth, whose phantoms I detest
I feel my stupid shit obscures
The purity my eyes long for
Why is there such an iconic split
Between the body and the brain?
My hungry head wanders, fit
As a pit in its corporeal shell
I keep banging on the bars
Trying to break out of my mental cage
I want to die / be born again
Torn apart, beating against
The walls of two mismatched worlds

Here's my lifelong anthem:
"My love, why do you send me so high
You're so hot, you hit the spot
But why do you tempt me to know
So many things that can't be explained?"
You looked in my eyes, you captured my head,
Took it on one long blazing phantasmagoric trip
The voyages never let up, my passport stamped
For multiple entries
Into the freedom-loving country of your body

My body only belongs to me
I'm a traveling man — or woman
I live in a country like yours
Where the needs of the body have always ruled
But I will never bow, never submit
I'll say "No!" until my brain sweats
I won't let myself be taunted or teased
So I move at night along the highways
There are flashes of magnesium
Shadows stumble over death. Darkness
Drapes love. Cracked lips sync

Starved words. What is the meaning
Of this silence? Is it fear or love
That has shuttered the eyes?
I'm weary with desire but this old ox head
Will stumble on,
The cart of the body creaking after

I'm a masquerade man, a man with a mask
A knife in one hand, a mirror in the other
A malevolent man with a face to match
Fueled by lust seeking random objects of desire
No need for transcendence, or impulse to go higher
Let the night come, let the chaos begin
Take a look at my eyes
They populate hundreds of city streets
I'm not different from you, you're no different from me
We both blaze for a bit in planetary darkness

Searchlight eyes pivoting, wheeling, turning, searching
For a sign of that intangible something

We go wandering with our weapons in the wilderness

If you're looking for a proof of God
I can only offer my pain
You can benchmark the agony
By what is bladed deep in the gut
Wrap your arms a hundred times
Around this bandaged head
A life lost will never console the dead

But is it enough, is it enough if you long to escape
From the bourgeois routine
Of mashed potatoes and ice cream?
From the cinders of lives destroyed before they began?

Dark rows of heads line up in the cinema
Gasping at flickering phantoms
Thousands of one-eyed fish spiraling
Down through shards of plastic
Dead at the bottom of the Pacific

Beer can heads, you smell, you've seen too much,
You stink of life!
If only you could have remained true to yourself,
The inner vision, the joyful eye of the child
If you couldn't accept the future that was bound to happen
Why couldn't you just have screamed "NO!"?

Instead you let the beautiful dreams die
Your forehead thumb pressed to a smudge
Death came for you, dancing in the mud and the muck
No wonder you grimaced
From deep in your belly howled "Fuck!"
The ecstasy you sought in love was finally
Just another way of creaming yourself

There was no way out of your head
No exit
From the revelatory horoscope of your eyes

In the black hour of naked neurons, of cellular memories
When thoughts, inverting, sink below the sea level
Of the brain, then elevated above the body
Beyond oblivion, the incubator head gravitates

Persists beyond the dreams of the flesh, strange
Shimmers of gold lurk behind the eyes
Hints of a vanished radiance, thus it is

And what is, is now no more, slipping away,
Jumping off point into galaxies
Your flying atoms reshaped into stars

The control tower still sits calmly on your neck

The great beams rotate, blasting

Imaginary points of perspective in the brain

For more than two thousand years we have listened

To the spoken/unspoken songs of the human head

Rage, rancor, anger, lust, madness, think of all the crazy

Woozy feelings buzzing like a hornet's nest

If only we could learn to be silent, alone in a room

Or in the beauty of a reclining woman find our rest

Dear God, Who is not in heaven and certainly not on earth

Please help me to break out of my shell head

My poor peanut of a body

Using the only weapon I have: my egg teeth

Or hit the target of universal truth

With a well-guided phallic arrow

If emptiness is form, form emptiness

To the threat of shapelessness

I raise my nose in defiance like a middle finger

Or help me to find a balance
Between dueling demands of head and body
In a Zen state of zero

Dear head, with your bold, bright, blank eyes
Fixated on something else since you suffered
And rose from the dead
From the ashes of one woman's love
And of all the other past/future loves
With your parched tongue, thirsty for knowing
What it was not given to you to know
For the half-heard echoes trapped for all time
Between your ears, and your lips longing to utter
What it was never vouchsafed to them to utter
The root of all this wanting goes far back
To man's desire for the earth-born mother

While helmeted heads goosestep to the tune of the Mutterland
On funeral pyres by the river starved skulls crack and explode

Prince Hamlet, balanced on a hyphen of lonely
In his empire of emptiness, also held one, pondered
If the brief game was worth the tapered candle

Hey ding a ding, the little birds still sing in the spring
Time like a river will flow with your golden hair
My beautiful Shulamite, you with no blame
On the throne of bare shoulders your royal head reigns

In the breath of chaos, in the forest of our darkness
We lit a fire and played life wildly
Lips joined seamlessly
In one mad eternal epiphany of a kiss

Nose to nose, dear darling, isn't that how it was
When we were breathless and didn't give a damn
About the world and all the primeval shit
Silhouettes of our heads merged together
In a single forever frame

From crates of garbage rotting on the sidewalk
We found and saved one strawberry

Every night my yoyo head
Unreels as far as the moon
But in the morning
The body jerks it back

If this life is only a test

Why do I flounder and fail

I'm such a twerk

The dome of my head cursed

From the moment it emerged

Between her forked thighs

Into the daylight emergency

My face now full frontal

Head shaven, no bandage

Blindfold or hood, balanced

On the brink of light and darkness

Expressing itself well

With neither eroticism

Or mysticism, simply working out

Through the dimensions of

Eyes, nose, ears, mouth

The wonder of its essence

Shush, my lips

There's no need to talk

We already know everything

You can remove the headphone wires

The true song sings inside

No need of any more idols
There are enough skies
Reflected in your eyes

Interesting how the mind balks
When it hits hard against
The earth red rock of reality
The lips ache
From the pain of too much useless talk
You stay silent while you wait
For the lungs to expand
At the thought of too much beauty
Meanwhile you study hard to graduate
From the day and night school of uncertainty
It's hungry, it's hurt, it cries out
As relentlessly it is put to the test
The solitary head remains blessed
After all, how much time on this planet is left?
Time ticks by, shattered metronome
What's left is a bitter lemon leaf of life
You never reckoned would come to pass
You threw it away, watched as it fluttered
Drifting merrily, merrily down the stream

Suppose you cast a fishing line
Into the still waters of time
What would you expect to catch?
A sudden scarlet leaping fish of love?
Or some dreadful octopus memory dredged
From subconscious subterranean depths?

Inside the vault of the head lie hidden
The terrible truths of prehistoric events
How sweet to live in spite of everything,
To surge, to soar, to fly!

You stare straight ahead, impenetrable regard
Your eyes fighting hard not to sink
Under the weight of what they've seen

The music of the mind has wings

What cannot ever be understood is what
You never stop trying to understand

At age of eighteen you skipped town, flew
The coup without giving a damn, giving
A finger to all the Mama boys in the band

You kept your head just above water

You felt lucky

It didn't end up in a noose in the cellar

Remember how a long time ago

In the birth void of time

Breathless, choked

An umbilical cord around the neck

Bonjour, my head

To go away, to lose myself in a disappearing distance

As geared up to survive

As a fist jammed into a pocket

I travelled to the tune of splendid loves

Seeking a heavenly crotch

I could bury my lonely head deeply within

My sex stood out like a thorn

That happened to be stuck on my body

I sniffed and searched for mesmerizing scents

With the two straw vacuum of my nose

In a field of crushed hopes, my bulldozed ears

I knew one day death would catch me

In its crimson vertigo

Mocked by my own laughter, I suspended
Mirrors in my cage, so I could sing tender
Love songs to myriad reflections of myself

When I was twenty-one my father disowned me
He said he knew the moment I was born
Whatever I did was destined to be crap
Now you see why it was never easy
To find a reasonable place for myself on the map

Between the inner and the outer
The sensation and the perceived
The intuition and the form
Between the head and the body
Our miniscule "I", what makes me "me"
Captured in mid-flight
A bird to be, and yet "not yet"
Adrift like a feather in a chaos of chance
In the deep silence at the heart of things
Aware that all the days lived and loved
Belong to a never-finished ending
Seeking to salvage the one word

That might signify something

Unlocking the key, smaller than a penny

To the inner mystery

From my eyes to your lips, to write this

One hundred billion neurons networked in the brain

Spark improbable thoughts, linking

Time past, blood-red memories, an ever-lingering

Longing for a future never to be, amazingly

The seeds of a universe contained

Within the jellied sponge of the cerebellum

So, crippled by life, you lie sprawled with your books gathered

Around you on your phantastic monastic bed

When you caress the spines, prying open the pages

You feel you are touching something electric, alive

Which is why you hug them so close

All those imagined feelings endlessly enlarging your head

What you are looking for is simpler than you think

Perhaps can be found in the outstretched palm of a child's hand

Meanwhile you seek to escape from the cell

Of your image-shooting, repetitive skull

To fly, to float, to flash! Spitting out syllables
Like bullets, if you're not careful
You'll lose your hat!
You'll lose yourself!
You'll get knocked down, nose pressed
Against the earth. You'll be solemn, sealed
With the luxury of what life
Has done to you, and silent
As a baby sung to sleep

It's true: the heart has rooms for happiness
The shrunken head will never know
The joy it feels is almost marital
A body-wedded, flesh-bonded bliss
Sometimes it takes a long time to realize the meaning
Of one true deeply felt kiss

Lying in bed at night, feeling the dark of the darkness
Eyes riveted on dream image,
The head, fine flower, trembling with desire
On the fragile neck stalk
Everything waves, vibrates, even the heart
Is thrumming, but you are neither hero or poet
But a prey to the lure of fugitive thoughts

A past beyond recall, emotions that flash
Briefly as mica. The eyes stammer
In the haze, the ambiguous obscurity
Of the warm light, and the head goes on trembling
Before the tangled tremoring, life

Not long ago you could have made the big decisions
That could have changed the way your vision slanted
On a certain day, but giving yourself to love
You gave it all away, sorrow could either flatten
Your head like a coin, or the simplest happiness
Make it explode like a grape

Or shattered by a bullet, a plume of blood

Dark eyes stare out, darker eyes stare in
Searching the unknown in the depths within
If only, even once, they could see themselves
So the "be" of the body could survive its becoming

Horseshoe head, framed by time,
Like a fist clenching fire,
Eyes full of a somber lucidity
Lips tight with taciturnity

Ears jutting out like wings
Of sun-polished stone
Our civilization of tissue paper and hell
Did nothing to smooth or shape
It is life that is constantly codifying it
Into the great untouchable roundness
Of its mineral forms

Holding my head, enfolding my arms
Around the emptiness of the pain

There's a strange mix of energy and ecstasy
I will never get beyond

Is it as simple as saying that we are voluntary victims
Of a woman's raspberry lips? How heavy they can be!
Voluptuous truck carrying their cargo
Of mystery into the night of our tongues
As, pendulum, we swing back and forth
Buffeted by passion from one blood redness to another

It's true I'm not yet dead yet
But that doesn't mean I'm alive
Standing stock still

I let my breath do the talking
It flows in and out, brings
Me back to a nameless center
In the blue-black book of endless things
Instead of beating my head
Against a headboard, or squeezing
My head in my hands till it hurts
I want to let it return to the cool
Free fullness of what it once was
At one with itself
Then at last I will be free
My eyes will stop staring, begin to see
And what they see will be a remembrance
Of what they saw before

Count your breath
Let each breath be a year
Exhale, watch how quickly each one dies
You are left with the emptiness of form
Which is the same as the fullness of being

Your mind makes a move, floats out the window
You try to grab it —
It's already lost in space

I will go on holding my head in my hands
The one real thing that I can touch
Ears tuned to the songs within

But the primal guilt remains
My head and body split, axed
Each read different texts of desire
When will the promised day come
When they merge into peaceful one?

It is evening now — one by one all the lights
In the house of my head turn on
There is early darkness in the streets
The eyes stare out hard but do not see
Then the moonlight comes, so strong
It almost blinds, in the solitude
You've come to call your own
You turn away, you hand-shade your face

Your face is like my face, can be replaced
By any face, and love, when it is good
Is also faceless, because there is no way to name
All the invisible shapes our bodies trace
In that timeless time of no place

It's true I've lost my head to you
I look at you downside up, reversed in two
Head over heels in love with you
I would gladly exchange the rest of my fate
For a life-long glimpse of your ephemeral face

A woman like you is the magical myth in the mind
That centuries ago launched a thousand ships
Look, this head has grown horns, I'm a minotaur man!
In that legendary labyrinth of lust —
One powerful, convulsive thrust
You gasp, you cry, you whimper and moan
You knock your head hard against mine
Exploding my mind

Thus it is, from the hurt and the pain
From the battle of blood, concentrated energy
Like the stream of a fighter jet
We pilot our way into the stratosphere
Until we crash into God, bull's eye

To reach that moment I had to wait
For such a long time on the ground
My head bled
With the memory of losses of all my dead

Battered head, aching eyes, dumb tongue
Longing to unscramble the wild words,
The holy alphabet of life

You can cut off my head but you will never kill me
I will love you until my eyes can no longer see

They say two heads are better than one
But if you could join your head with mine
Mate my mind with yours
So that your dreams and mind are mine too
Then surely one conjoined mind is better than two

Since at best we're guests
Called away at a moment's fling
I often think of doing it myself
To control destiny extinguish the energy
And break beyond —
Only way to escape
Finding peace is the ultimate test

I poke a finger in my eye
I gaze a razor along my wrist

I tweak my ear, I pound my rage
The violence I feel has no age
It comes from the root of deepest anger
Here's the crux:
First I largely lived
Then I loudly loved
All the while knowing I have to die
It might even be all right
If I knew there was some other way out
But I fear the worst —
There is no breathing without air
If we were lovers in life
We will be brothers and sisters in death
The shared ecstasy of beauty or sex
Is no consolation for the big black X
I twist and turn as I envision ashes in an urn
Let it be known I sought to live life big
The darkness to come will make me small
So no surprise I take this goddamn head
And bang it again and again against the wall

Pig-headed me. I flounder, fail and fall

But in your love I will rise again

Ashes will become petals in the wind
And so we go on, holding my head
In your hands, holding your head in mine
We will fall into flying

Nuestra Senora de la Santa Muerte
Lady patron of our ecological extinction
I can't wait for your promise to manifest
Returning the land to the animals that own it
In the meantime I prowl every night on my own
Hurling dreams against windows like curses

When I am no longer here
I don't want my skeleton to owe debts to death
So burn this body on a pyre as saffron-
Robed monks do on the steps of the Ganges
Pay attention to the champagne sound
When my head finally bursts and goes pop

So much better than coping with decay and rot!

But death might be so boring and I don't want to die
I want to know again the taste of your sweat
My cathedral lady of the multicolored shadows

How the virgin light leaps like a fish along your brow
Some passionate pest has bitten your neck
So many openings, ears, smeared lips
So much space, time, fire, memory and man

Clutching my hollow head in my hands

Evening bells tell it's time to bed myself alone
First kneel to the memory of one love, final losses
While in the night sky the eye of Horus surveys
A pair of giant rabbits romping in starry fields

You can blindfold and hood me and hang me
But you can never take away the light of my life

I will be the prophet of my own doom,
I have a trumpet that blossoms out of my ear
I'm a fool in the shape of a face
Propped on stilts I walk stiff as a machine
Matchstick thin
I'd like to jump back into high school, frolic
With baseballs bats and dirty sneakers
I'm singer, symbol and sacrifice
Of this spinning center of madness
The uncontrolled center of a poet's head

Have the courage to raise your dream-spattered head
Look hard and long at the sky
Let all that blue launder your eyes

Why is it that in the daily battle of the body
Between raw instincts and the mannered mind
Only the female in me survives?

When the physical self comes back
From the glorious hunt of the days
The head sits down and smiles
With the fruit of all that it has gathered
Yet I still worry about the Neanderthal man
Who haunts the unlit caves

But I'm not going to apologize for what I've done
Or haven't done
In this vale of tears and sadness
On this trail of joy and *amour fou* madness

One day it's true I'll be old
I'll stare out of an ancestor's gilded frame
My skin wrinkled like the ass of an elephant

But it will take a long time to efface
How you twisted strands around your finger
The many years I longed for the tender touch
In the tendrils of your maiden hair

Now undo your eyes —
All the masks of your "me" —
There will never be
More darkness
In darkness than this
Yet from somewhere deep inside
Beyond all the shadows
Of a vanished now
The blackness gleams

If you could see with your ears
Hear with your eyes
Whisper with your nose
Understand with your heart
Feel with your mind
If you could keep death away
If you could be happy alone
If you could linger a little longer in love

Erase the telltale signs on your face
If you knew the woman you loved would wait
If you could learn how to staunch the ache

Living in terror of the day when at last
I will come face to face with my face
Eye to eye with my own mortality
No more sound to the flat line
Lips, nostrils, cheeks and chin defined
In a mask of absolute finality
I pray there will be some forgiving or grace
That my head with its heft of half-lived dreams
Will not simply be eclipsed like a moon
In some easily forgotten hospital room

Lord, have pity on this simple, humble, sinful head
That once crowned from a crack between a mother's legs

I just want to be close to you again
Hooked up to the warmth of your earth and leaves
Nozzles of light illuminate the fine
Features of your holy face
Cleaning the grime of time
From centuries ago the seated Egyptian scribe
Continues to stare, to ask who we are?

Or should I simply reply, “Ego, Scriptor”?

So the poet in me reaches out to the reader in you

Hoping we can triangulate —

Ear to ear, eye to eye, head to head

THE HEAD, ENCORE

Bands of light sweep across
The forehead, the cheeks bathed
In silence, a hawk nose crowded
With familiar/unfamiliar scents
Column, the swarthy neck sinks
Beneath a jutting bearded chin
A loosely wrapped package of memories
The head reveals itself to time —

It flows, it goes to where nobody knows!
But the heavy head clings to life
Before it becomes the skull
Cookie- crumbling to dust
In the meantime, the shining
In between time, it remembers
The golden tunnel of summer afternoons

What regrets remain, what longing in the eyes
That never want to say goodbye?
Like a little boy the head sits on the shoulder
Endeavors to catch and keep

The endless parade floating by

    When I am dead be quiet if you walk
    About my head or the echo
    Of footsteps will scare it away

    Stretched taut on tiptoe, my ballerina lover
    You strain to hear
    Some words I might have left behind

At birth I sensed my life would be nothing
But my wise Mama said
"Even nothing is always something."

Later when I lurched into love
The roof of my head blew open
Thoughts escaping in spirals
Yet where were the roots?
Buried in the ground, in mud and graffiti

But it has the same light as before,
Has preserved the identical defiance
The whole face forming a subtle
System of mirrors. Think of the madness
Reflected within it, the big eyes

Bug-eyed, staring at you
Wondering about your point of origin

The roots of time grow deep in the mind
Dark whispers reverberate between the ears
How much can a brain weigh?
Gravity is always pulling it down
Pupils burning bright with intensity
Like the ebony navel of the Buddha
While my weightless thoughts seek to soar
What swerves, what arcs, what curves!

So yes, my head, unless you cast off
Your psychological clothes
Tomorrow will be exactly the same as today
And we will go on paired together
With a thousand more yeses

You'll sit in the autumn on a park bench
A scarf of sunshine over your shoulders
Me thinking: I wish my head were a door
So I could open and close it
Letting thoughts
In
If I liked them

Out

If I didn't

It is the mind that ceaselessly tries to bind

All the leaves scattered through the universe

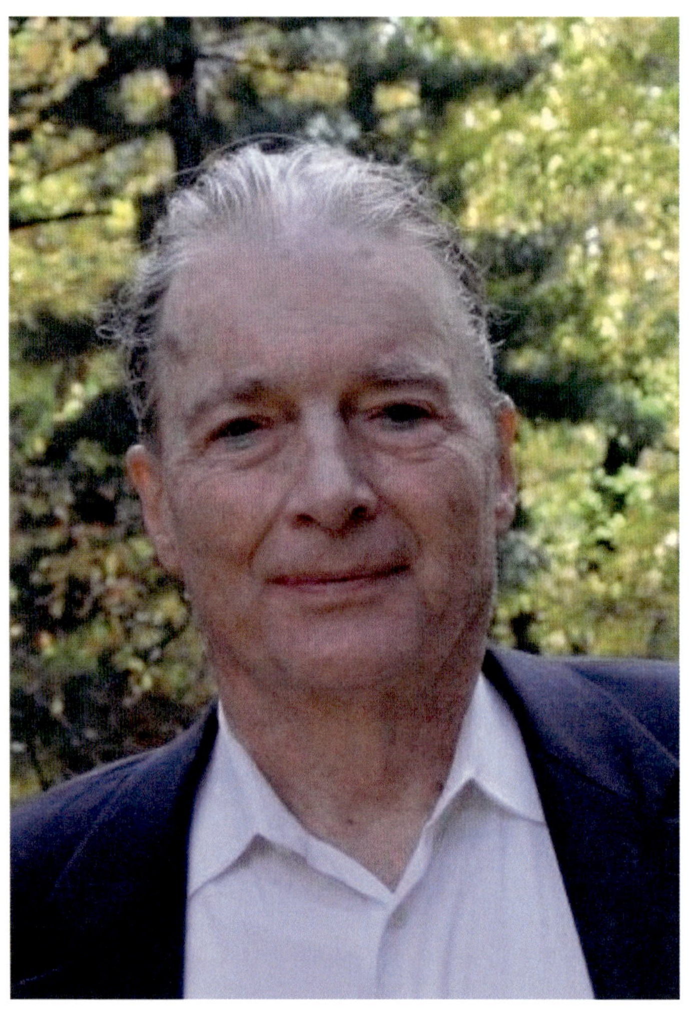

Wade Stevenson lives in Buffalo, NY

Made in the USA
Lexington, KY
23 November 2019

57465737R00043